Contents

Death of a President

The morning of 22 November 1963 was bright and warm. A line of twelve cars moved slowly through the streets of Dallas, in Texas. In one of these was John Kennedy, President of the United States, laughing and waving at the crowds who lined the route.

Suddenly, three rifle shots were heard. The President fell forward into the arms of his wife. He had been hit in the head and back.

His driver rushed him to the nearest hospital, four miles away. But it was too late. After less than three years in office, John Kennedy was dead, cut down by an assassin's bullets.

This tragedy shook the world. In America and Europe people cried in the streets. A Soviet newsreader broke down in tears. In Berlin, a candle-lit procession paid homage to the President. Rarely has the death of one man been mourned by so many people all over the world.

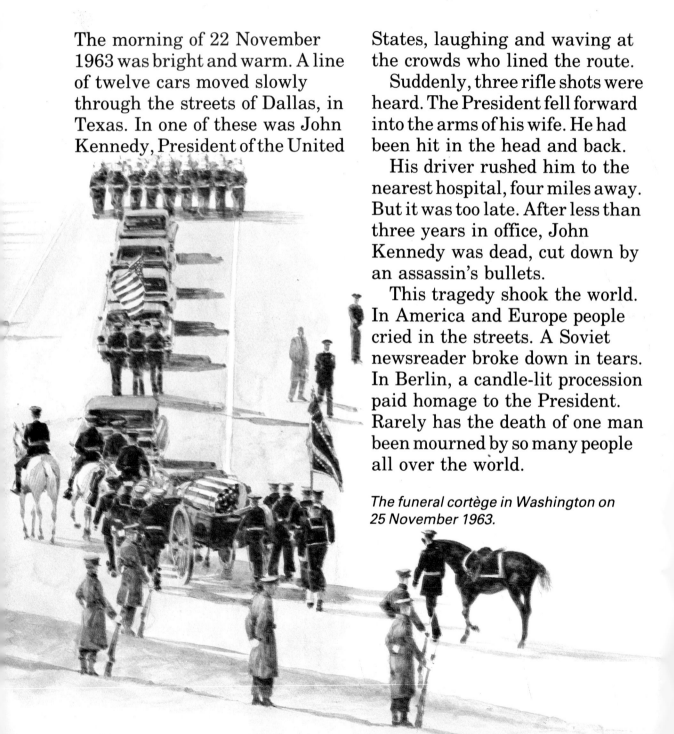

The funeral cortège in Washington on 25 November 1963.

John F. Kennedy

Andrew Langley

Illustrations by Richard Hook

Wayland

Great Lives

William Shakespeare
Queen Elizabeth II
Anne Frank
Martin Luther King
Helen Keller
Ferdinand Magellan
Mother Teresa
Louis Braille
John Lennon
John F. Kennedy
Florence Nightingale
Elvis Presley

First published in 1985 by
Wayland (Publishers) Limited
61 Western Road, Hove
East Sussex BN3 1JD, England

British Library Cataloguing in Publication Data
Langley, Andrew
    John F. Kennedy. – (Great Lives)
    1. Kennedy, John F. (John Fitzgerald)
    2. Presidents – United States – Biography
    I. Title   II. Hook, Richard   III. Series
    973.922′092′4   E842.Z9

    ISBN 0–85078–655–X

Phototypeset by Kalligraphics Ltd, Redhill, Surrey
Printed in Italy by G. Canale & C.S.p.A., Turin
Bound in Great Britain at The Bath Press, Avon

The second son

John Fitzgerald Kennedy was born on 29 May 1917, in a rambling house in Boston, Massachusetts. His parents, Joe and Rose, both came from important Irish-American families, the Kennedys and the Fitzgeralds.

His father was a shrewd and tough businessman who, through buying and selling companies, had become a millionaire several times over. He was also a strong supporter of the Democratic Party and a close friend of many politicians, including the future President Roosevelt.

Jack, the Kennedy's second son, at the age of six months.

The nursery where the Kennedy children spent their early years.

John, or Jack as he was fondly known, had been born two years after his elder brother Joseph. Over the next decade the Kennedy family grew rapidly. In all, there were nine children, five daughters and four sons. The youngest were Robert and Edward.

Family life

Young Jack grew up in an atmosphere of wealth and comfort. At the centre of the family was his mother Rose, a quiet, calm woman who brought up her children with devoted care. She listened to their problems, kept close track of their illnesses and taught them to take a keen interest in the affairs of the world. Being a devout Roman Catholic, she also encouraged them to attend church services.

It was a house buzzing with activity too. Jack's father had to deal with a stream of telephone calls, urgent letters and important visitors. Politics and business matters took up most of his time and he was often away from home. When he was there, all his energy went into playing with his children. It wasn't just play, either. Joe was determined that wealth should not make his family spoilt and lazy, and he made sure that they all quickly learned how tough the world could be.

Joseph and Rose Kennedy with eight of their nine children. (Jack is top left)

Their father organized family games of football, tennis and golf, and took them swimming and sailing. The children had to compete against each other – girls against boys, elder against younger. This constant rivalry between the brothers and sisters

'Policeman' Jack playing in the garden with one of his sisters.

The Kennedy family house, No. 83 Beals Street, Boston. It is now a museum.

produced a fierce will to win, which was to stay with Jack all his life.

At the dinner table, only the discussion of serious topics was allowed. 'If you didn't talk about world affairs, you just didn't talk', recalls a friend. The children joined in the arguments with great gusto because – as in everything else – they wanted to come out on top.

In the mid-1920s, the Kennedy family moved to the Bronx area of New York. By this time, Jack was a fervent reader. He was thrilled by stories of chivalry and adventure, particularly the deeds of King Arthur and his knights.

School and college

Jack is pictured (bottom right) in the school football team.

Jack was taught at various private schools, first in Boston and later in New York. But he never had great success at school, being especially bad at mathematics and spelling. However, he struggled on, with all the great Kennedy determination.

Two circumstances hampered Jack in his struggle. One was his big brother Joe. Handsome, charming, athletic and bright, Joe passed all his exams with ease, and was held up as a shining example to Jack. This saddened the younger boy, who felt that he was a disappointment to his father.

The other problem was his

health. As a child, Jack was often ill and once, at boarding school, he had to be rushed to hospital for an appendicitis operation. Later, while studying in England, he suffered an attack of jaundice and had to return home.

On the sports field, too, he could never quite match up to Joe. Being less well-built, he was never very good at football. But he kept trying, until one day his back was badly sprained by a hard tackle. The injury was never to heal completely.

It was at Harvard University that Jack first became interested in politics. He was inspired by his college course on government, and by a trip he took to Europe in 1937. There he saw the effects of the Fascist dictatorships in Italy, Germany and Spain, and came to realize that war could not be far away.

In the same year, his father was appointed United States Ambassador to Great Britain. Jack travelled to spend his holidays from Harvard in his parents' country house near London. By now, his university career was flourishing, and in 1940 he graduated with the highest honours.

Graduation day at Harvard University.

War hero

Even before the United States entered the Second World War in 1941, Jack had enlisted for the Navy. He was desperate to see action, and volunteered to train with the squadrons of 'PT-boats'. These were light and fast torpedo boats which, after war was declared, were used to harass Japanese ships in the Pacific.

The Kennedys were all experienced sailors so Jack had little trouble in qualifying for the course. But he had to wait another year before he was sent on combat duty. He was stationed in the Solomon Islands, in charge of a boat numbered PT 109. This boat was soon to become a legend.

The PT-boats patrolled a stretch of water called Blackett Strait, on the lookout for Japanese supply ships. Many of the nearby islands were held by the Japanese, and the American aim was to prevent food getting through to them.

The night of 1 August 1943 was pitch black. Without radar, PT 109 was cautiously making her way up Blackett Strait. Suddenly the giant shape of a Japanese destroyer loomed out of the darkness and sliced the small boat in two. Jack and his crew were left clinging to the wreckage.

Under Jack's command, they set out to swim for a small island, over three miles away. Jack himself towed a wounded man, pulling him with a strap held in his teeth. His back was aching and he swallowed mouthfuls of seawater, but he did not give up.

After a rest, he left the others ashore and swam out to look for help. All night he trod water, but no boats came near. He returned to the island, and eventually, on 5 August, two natives in a canoe spotted them. Jack scratched a message on a coconut shell for them to carry to the nearest friendly island. Two days later the exhausted survivors were rescued, thanks largely to the indomitable spirit of their leader.

Jack photographed in US naval uniform.

The reluctant Congressman

Jack emerged from the war a hero, but his ordeal in the sea had permanently damaged his back. He had also picked up malaria, a serious disease which left him gaunt and yellow-skinned. A far worse blow came in 1944, when his brother Joe was killed in a mid-air explosion.

Joe Jr, whose death so dramatically affected his brother's life.

Father and son discuss the prospects.

The tragedy stunned the Kennedys, who had held such high hopes for this talented and handsome man. Now Jack felt the weight of his father's dreams falling on to his shoulders.

After working for some months as a journalist, it was suggested to Jack that he should stand for election to Congress. The thought terrified him at first. He remembered vividly his failures at school and college, and in spite of his wartime experiences he was still shy and reserved. Also, he knew nothing about making speeches or organizing election campaigns.

becoming a popular figure on Capitol Hill. The voters of Boston liked him too, and they re-elected him twice more, in 1948 and 1950.

During this period, a second tragedy struck the family. Kathleen, Jack's favourite sister, was killed in an air crash in France. This was a bitter blow to Jack, and he pushed himself even harder at work to try to overcome his loss.

The triumphant young Congressman with his proud parents and grandmother, after his election to Congress in 1946.

Eventually, Jack's father talked him round, and once he decided to stand for Congress, Jack threw himself heart and soul into the election. It was not long before he overcame his shyness, and soon he was pounding the streets, knocking on doors and asking the people of Boston to vote for him. When polling day came he won easily, with more than twice as many votes as anyone else.

When the new Congressman arrived in Washington, he looked so young and skinny that he was mistaken for a schoolboy. However, he soon settled in, gaining in self-confidence and

The Senate and beyond

Now that he was launched on a political career, Jack took the obvious Kennedy course – straight towards the top. By 1952, he had decided to take his next step and stand as a Senator for the state of Massachusetts.

Many members of the Democratic Party were shocked by the speed of his rise and the style of his

vote-catching. His campaign headquarters was run by his brother Bobby, who was only twenty-seven years old. The rest of the staff were also young and inexperienced. However, they worked ceaselessly. Jack travelled all over Massachusetts

Jack conferring with his young brother Bobby.

talking to voters, with barely time to stop for meals. His injured back could not stand the strain, and in the end he had to walk on crutches. But the result was worth all his efforts – he defeated his opponent by 70,000 votes and became one of the two Senators for the state of Massachusetts.

Shortly after this triumph, he married twenty-four-year-old Jacqueline Lee Bouvier, a journalist and daughter of a wealthy family from Rhode Island.

Jack plunged into his work at the Senate with all his usual energy but, by the autumn of 1954, his back condition became so bad that he required operations. Following the operations, he had to spend many weeks lying flat in bed. But Jack used this time to write a book about American politics which quickly became a bestseller.

When Jack returned to the Senate he was greeted with applause from all the other Senators. He was now becoming known as a national figure in the United States, although most of the bills (proposals) which he introduced in the Senate were still concerned with local issues in

The wedding of Jack and Jacqueline.

Massachusetts.

Now it was time to take the third step in his career. But, to Jack's dismay, he failed to be chosen as the candidate for Vice-President in the election of 1956. However, two years later, he was returned to the Senate with an even greater number of votes than before.

President of the United States

Senator Kennedy's massive victory made him one of the best-known Democrats in the country, and an obvious candidate for the Presidency in 1960. This time he had no difficulty in being chosen by his party at their National Convention in Los Angeles. He picked the Texan Senator Lyndon Johnson to campaign with him as candidate for the Vice-Presidency.

Jack's Republican opponent was Richard Nixon, an experienced and wily politician. In his speeches, Nixon made the most of what seemed to be the Democrat's weak points. He was very young for a possible President – barely more than forty years old. Jack had very little knowledge of political power. Moreover, he was a Roman Catholic: no Catholic had

John F. Kennedy takes the oath of office as 35th President of the United States.

The new President in his office at the White House.

ever been President.

Realizing that even he could not cover the entire country during his campaign, Jack concentrated on the states of the North-East. He followed an exhausting routine, snatching a few hours of sleep on planes and gulping down hot dogs and soup when he could.

The turning point came when both men agreed to appear in public debates on television. Before an audience of more than seventy million Americans, the two politicians answered questions and outlined their policies. It was clear from the start that Jack was better informed, more relaxed and wittier than his opponent.

On election night, the Kennedys and their team sat nervously watching the results coming in on television. By early morning, the final count showed a small majority for Jack. The new President, who had gone to bed tired out, had to be roused and told the great news.

Two months later, the youngest President in American history took the oath of office. With his wife and family – three year-old Caroline and baby John – he moved into the White House, the last home he would ever have.

The New Frontier

Jack chose the moment of his inauguration to make an inspiring speech to his fellow-citizens. 'Let the word go forth,' he said, 'from this time and place to friend and foe alike, that the torch has been passed to a new generation of Americans – born in this century, tempered by war, disciplined by a hard and bitter peace.'

The new President was echoing the spirit of the times. Americans were tired of a plodding government which had done little to cure the great problems of the day – poverty and racial hatred. The shadow of nuclear war with the Soviet Union hung over the nation.

During his election campaign tours of America, Jack had

The police using fire hoses on civil rights marchers in the South.

become increasingly aware of the problems facing the country. He had seen children suffering from lack of food, and the despair of unemployed men and women. He had been saddened by the harsh treatment of black people, especially in the South where they were regarded as inferior beings. Now, as President, he spoke of 'The New Frontier', where the war against these evils could be fought.

A Peace Corps, consisting of young volunteers, was formed to help countries in Africa, Asia and Latin America. These young people volunteered to spend two

Caroline and John running in to see their father in his White House office.

years in the poorer countries, helping with teaching, engineering, medical services and many other urgently needed skills. The nearby Latin American nations were also aided and encouraged to help sort out their economic difficulties, and were granted funds by the United States Treasury.

This fresh and energetic approach could be seen, too, in the White House. The Kennedys treated it as their home and not just as the President's official dwelling. Conferences and interviews were likely to be interrupted by Caroline or young John bouncing through the door. Jack could be seen playing golf in the gardens. His wife Jackie supervised the redecoration of many stuffy old rooms.

An early disaster

The new President had made a stirring start to his term of office. Young Americans, delighted to be given some responsibility, were clamouring to join the Peace Corps. The newspapers were full of praise. Letters of encouragement poured into the White House. But Jack was soon to suffer a major setback.

A few years earlier, in 1959, the island of Cuba had been taken over by a Communist

President Kennedy talking to young volunteers of the Peace Corps.

revolutionary government led by Fidel Castro. The United States were alarmed to find a Communist stronghold less than 160 kilometres (100 miles) from their shores. Eisenhower, the President at the time, had devised a secret plan to invade Cuba and overthrow Castro, using a specially-trained force of Cuban exiles.

It was a shock for Kennedy to discover that this plan was to be put into operation only three months after he had taken office as President. He decided against cancelling the invasion, but he made sure that no American soldiers would take part in the fighting.

The landing, at the Bay of Pigs, was a complete fiasco. There was no support from the Cuban people and the exiles were soon killed or captured. It was scarcely Jack's fault, for he had inherited the project from his predecessor, yet he insisted on accepting all the blame for the failure.

All the same, it was a blow to his pride. Jack determined to learn his lesson and make sure

United States

Cuba

SOUTH
AMERICA

that, if ever a similar venture was planned, it would be properly organized. He also began to realize that brute force was rarely the best way of dealing with a problem.

America's biggest problem, of course, was the need for an end to the arms race with the Soviet Union. The President was anxious that a treaty to limit the numbers of nuclear weapons should be agreed between the two countries. The disaster in Cuba, however, seemed to make such a treaty unlikely.

21

A symbol of hope

The President and Mr Khrushchev meeting in Vienna to discuss a ban on nuclear tests.

Just a month after the Bay of Pigs disaster, the President was surprised and delighted to learn that the leader of the Soviet Union, Nikita Khrushchev, was willing to talk with him. The two men met in Vienna and discussed many important issues, including the banning of nuclear weapon tests. Mr Khrushchev had come expecting to be able to bully Kennedy, but he was quickly impressed by the young President's toughness and by his charm.

The President made a favourable impression on many people. To the young of America he was a symbol of hope and progress. Being still young himself, he got things done – fast. He could read reports at 1200 words a minute and grasp all the details: he had no patience with long-winded explanations.

The President was determined to see justice done to his citizens and his determination was put to the test in April 1962. The big steelmaking companies asked for his help in persuading steel workers to settle for a small pay rise. They said that a big wage increase would raise the price of steel itself. Through Jack's influence, the workers agreed to the smaller pay rise. But it had all been a trick. Next day, the steel bosses announced that they were increasing the price of steel anyway! Jack was enraged. He made an angry speech attacking the bosses for their greed, and he soon had the support of members of the public, most of whom agreed with him. The steel companies had to climb down and admit defeat and steel prices remained as they were.

The President needed even more courage to tackle the problem of civil rights. Although slavery had been abolished a hundred years earlier, many black people still lived separate lives, especially in the southern states. They lived in the poorest, run-down areas, went to separate schools, and were despised by many white Americans.

Jack had pledged himself to help black Americans gain equal rights with white Americans. The opportunity to make a firm stand on this issue came in the summer of 1962. A negro student was being barred from the University of Mississippi because of his colour. To protect him from the angry crowds, Jack sent in federal troops.

Federal troops are sent to protect a black student in Mississippi.

The Cuban Missiles

The most dramatic and dangerous episode during President Kennedy's term of office began in September 1962. The government of the Soviet Union admitted that it was sending weapons to the Cubans, but insisted that they were only for defence purposes.

In October, a high-flying American plane took photographs of air bases on Cuba. These showed clearly that missiles with atomic warheads were being installed on the island. Experts worked out that these missiles could reach any city in the United States within a few minutes.

President Kennedy took immediate action. He knew that he must stand up to this threat and force the Soviets to withdraw their missiles. On the other hand, he had to be very careful not to provoke a nuclear war between the two countries.

He ordered the United States Navy to blockade Cuba and search all ships sailing into her ports. Then he sent a stern message to Premier Khrushchev, demanding that all the missiles should be removed from the

The busy President taking time off to be with his family.

island. A Russian cargo ship was stopped and searched by American destroyers, but was found to be carrying no weapons.

All the world held its breath, but the Soviet Union made no move for two whole days. At last, Khrushchev agreed to withdraw not only the missiles but also planes, rockets and troops. It was a humiliating defeat for the Russian leader, but his decision restored peace without any loss of life.

President Kennedy's firmness of purpose and tough talking during this frightening crisis had made him a hero to many people. This was the closest the world had yet come to a Third World War, but he had kept his nerve and forced the Russians to back down.

Talks with Moscow

The Cuban crisis was a sharp shock to the leaders of the two superpowers. They realized that such a dangerous confrontation must not be allowed to happen again.

Early in 1963, President Kennedy received a letter from Mr Khrushchev. The Russian Premier said that he was anxious to come to an agreement about the ending of nuclear tests. He was even prepared to allow Soviet bases to be inspected three times a year, to make clear that he was keeping to the bargain.

The Americans were delighted by this offer. For months, representatives of many nations had been in Geneva, discussing the ending of nuclear tests. They had been unable to agree on a treaty because the Soviet representatives had refused to allow inspections. Now, at last, the way for a settlement seemed clear.

After more weeks of argument, the Test-Ban Treaty was signed by the United States, the Soviet Union and Great Britain. All nuclear tests above ground, under water or in outer space were forbidden. However, test explosions could still be carried out underground. This was an historic moment.

There was another lesson to be learned from the missiles crisis. The two leaders must be able to talk directly to each other instead of using telegrams which took hours to reach their destinations. So a teletype 'hot-line' was set up between the leaders in Washington and Moscow.

These successes made Jack the most popular United States President for many years, both at home and abroad. In June 1963 he visited Berlin. The former German capital had been divided in two after the Second World War, and in 1961 the Russians had built a wall along the border to prevent people moving from East to West.

The citizens of West Berlin, cut off from the rest of their country, welcomed the United States President with great enthusiasm. Jack confirmed his support for them in a famous speech by declaring, 'I am a Berliner', and telling the world that if they wanted to see courageous people they should come to Berlin.

President Kennedy addressing the enthusiastic crowds in Berlin.

The last days

By the summer of 1963, Jack knew that it was time for him to start on the campaign trail for election once again. The next elections were due in a year's time, and all his successes in the past had depended on careful planning and a great deal of travelling throughout the country.

The opinion polls showed that he was almost certain to be elected for a second term of office. But Jack knew that most of his support came from the northern states. His programme of Civil Rights laws had made him very unpopular in the Deep South, so he decided to make his first trip to a southern state – Texas.

That spring, racial trouble had flared up again in Birmingham, Alabama. Demonstrations by black people, led by Martin Luther King, had been attacked by brutal policemen using dogs and truncheons. The President had sent a team to help restore peace. He had also announced new laws which would bring greater equality for negroes.

In the autumn, Jack and his wife set off on a tour of Florida and Texas. It was during the visit to Texas that the President was assassinated in the streets of Dallas. His killer was Lee Harvey Oswald, an unhappy and embittered man who had once lived in Moscow. Two days later, Oswald himself was shot dead by a night-club owner who claimed to be avenging the murder of the President.

The coffin of John Kennedy was flown to Capitol Hill in Washington, where his body lay in state for a day. During that time, thousands of Americans filed past the coffin, to pay their last respects to the man who had given them a new hope for the future. Then he was buried at

Lee Harvey Oswald takes careful aim and the hopes of a generation are shattered.

Arlington National Cemetery in Washington, and his widow lit an eternal flame in his memory.

It is as a young man that Kennedy is remembered today. His short term as President brought the promise of many things – relief from the threat of Cold War, freedom for the oppressed black people of America, and confidence in the future of the world. Had he lived, that promise might have faded. What will never fade is the memory of his youthful energy and idealism in an age when these were in short supply.

The heads of state of many nations were among the mourners at the President's funeral.

Important dates

1917   (29 May) Born in Boston, Massachusetts.

1930   Sent away to boarding school in Connecticut.

1935   Visit to London cut short by illness.

1936   Enrols for the University of Harvard.

1937   Jack's father appointed US Ambassador to Britain; Jack travels around Europe.

1939   Second World War breaks out.

1941   Enlists in the US Navy; America joins the war.

1943   Joins PT-Boat squadron in the Solomon Islands: his boat is sunk but he leads his crew to safety.

1944   Elder brother Joe killed.

1945   The war ends.

1946   Elected to Congress for the first time: re-elected 1948 and 1950.

1952   Becomes Senator for Massachusetts: re-elected 1958.

1953   Marries Jacqueline Lee Bouvier.

1954   Undergoes two operations on his back.

1955   Fails to gain the Democratic nomination as Vice-Presidential candidate.

1957   Daughter Caroline born.

1960   Chosen as Presidential candidate by his party: narrowly wins the Presidency over Richard Nixon. Son John born.

1961   Inaugurated as President and moves into the White House. The Bay of Pigs fiasco: first meeting with Khrushchev.

1962   Forces the steel companies to keep prices steady. Sends Federal troops to keep law and order in Mississippi. Wins prestige during Cuban Missiles Crisis.

1963   Nuclear Test-Ban Treaty agreed with the USSR: hot-line set up between Washington and Moscow. Announcement of a new Civil Rights Bill. Visits Berlin. (22 November) Assassinated in Dallas, Texas.

Books to read

Castro by Paul Humphrey (Wayland, 1981)

Kennedy by Elizabeth Campling (Batsford Educational, 1980)

Martin Luther King by Nigel Hunter (Wayland, 1985)

One Brief Shining Moment by William Manchester (Michael Joseph, 1983)

Portrait of a President by William Manchester (Michael Joseph, 1967)

Young Man in the White House by I. E. Levine (Bailey, 1970)

Glossary

Blockade To prevent ships from entering or leaving a port.

Capitol Hill The hill on which the Capitol, the main building of the United States Congress, stands.

Civil rights The rights due to all citizens of a country, including the right to vote and to be treated equally.

Cold War The rivalry between the Western World and the Soviet World, which, although often tense, stops short of real war.

Congress The national governing authority of the United States which passes laws, consisting of the Senate and the House of Representatives.

Communist A system of government under which all land, industry and commerce is owned by the state.

Deep South The south-eastern states of the USA, especially South Carolina, Georgia, Alabama, Mississippi and Louisiana.

Democratic Party One of the two major political parties in the USA. The other is the Republican Party.

Election campaign A programme of speeches and canvassing which an election candidate undertakes in order to win people's votes.

Fascist dictatorship A government which follows militaristic and nationalist policies and concentrates power in the hands of a few people.

Hot-line The direct teletype link set up in 1963 between Moscow and Washington, allowing the leaders of the USA and the USSR to communicate with each other during an emergency.

Inauguration The ceremony during which a new American President takes his oath of office.

Latin America The countries of Central and South America (including Mexico) where Spanish and Portuguese are spoken.

Nuclear tests The controlled explosion of nuclear bombs to see how effective they are.

Peace Corps Teams of young voluntary workers recruited to help people in poor countries of Africa, Asia and Latin America.

Senate The upper house of Congress in the USA: two Senators are elected from each state.

Superpowers Extremely powerful nations such as the USA and USSR.

Picture credits

Photographs on the following pages, 5 (lower), 7 (upper) are reproduced by kind permission of the National Park Service – John F. Kennedy NHS. All other photographs in the book and on the cover come from the John F. Kennedy Library, Boston, USA. Cover artwork is by Richard Hook.

Index